What Do You Know?

What
Do You
Know?

Tamela Hancock Murray

BARBOUR
PUBLISHING, INC.
Uhrichsville, Ohio

Published by Barbour Publishing, Inc., P.O. Box 719, Uhrichsville, OH 44683, http://www.barbourbooks.com

Member of the
Evangelical Christian
Publishers Association

Printed in the United States of America.

INTRODUCTION

Well, what do you know—biblically speaking?

You're about to find out! Welcome to *What Do You Know?* It's a trivia book that's not at all trivial—not when it covers the most important Book in all of human history. Scores of questions covering a number of Bible topics—everything from animals to miracles, from Genesis to Revelation—will test your scriptural mettle.

If you're new to the Christian faith, it's a fun introduction to some of the key characters and issues of the Scriptures. If you've been around for a while, it's a great way to brush up on some of those same topics. And if you're a Bible expert with all the answers, why not take the further challenge of providing verse references for each question?

So, what do you know? Read on to find out!

PROVERBIAL PEARLS

1. Who wrote Proverbs?

2. The Proverbs are written to impart wisdom to the:
   a. foolish virgin   c. newlywed
   b. young man   d. oppressed

3. "The fear of the _____ is the beginning of knowledge."

4. According to Proverbs, wisdom and instruction are despised by:
   a. the evil   c. fools
   b. young men   d. the rich

5. "For the turning away of the simple shall slay them, and the _____ of fools shall destroy them."

6. Wisdom is granted by Whom?

7. The strange woman and the stranger who flatters lead to:
   a. death   c. prosperity
   b. crime   d. false love

8. "Trust in the _____ with all thine heart; and lean not unto thine own understanding."

9. The Lord corrects whom?

10. True or False: Proverbs says that wisdom is better than rubies.

11. Proverbs 3:18 compares wisdom to:
    a. a sweet woman
    b. a flower in bloom
    c. aromatic spices
    d. a tree of life

12. The wise shall inherit:
    a. the promised land
    b. glory
    c. a good wife
    d. the first fruits of the father

13. True or False: Proverbs 4:13 compares instruction to life.

14. The sluggard should consider the ways of the:
    a. beaver   c. serpent
    b. ant   d. dove

15. "Drink waters out of thine own _____, and running waters out of thine own well."

16. Proverbs 5:18–21 explains what is meant by the admonition to drink from thine own well. What is the real wisdom behind this symbolism?

17. Proverbs 6:16–19 names seven things that are abominations to the Lord. How many can you name?

18. "The fear of the LORD is to hate _____."

19. True or False: Possessing wisdom will make you live longer.

20. True or False: Proverbs says stolen waters are sweet, and bread eaten in secret is pleasant.

21. Proverbs 10:20 says that the tongue of the just is as:
   a. choice silver   c. a flatterer
   b. sweet wine   d. flowing honey

22. True or False: The Lord will overlook the false balance of the faithful servant.

23. A talebearer revealeth:
    a. the truth   c. righteousness
    b. secrets   d. the light

24. True or False: There should be one coun-
    sellor to guide the people, lest there be
    dispute.

25. According to Proverbs 12:4, a virtuous
    woman is a:
    a. beauty to behold
    b. picture of frugality
    c. crown to her husband
    d. worthy mother

26. "Lying lips are _____ to the
    LORD: but they that deal truly are his
    delight."

27. What will happen to wealth gotten by
    vanity?

28. "He that spareth his _____ hateth his
    son: but he that loveth him chasteneth
    him betimes."

29. What type of answer turns away wrath?

30. What is your favorite proverb?

IT'S THE LAW, SON

1. Where in the Bible is the Mosaic law found?

2. Who wrote down the Old Testament laws?

3. True or False: A man was to be free at home for one year after marriage to be with his new wife.

4. What was the penalty for kidnapping?

5. "Remember the sabbath day, to keep it _____."

6. How old was a baby boy to be on the day of his circumcision?

7. True or False: A woman who had just given birth was considered unclean for a shorter period of time after the birth of a boy than after the birth of a girl.

8. How did God provide for the poor under the Mosaic law?

9. True or False: The admonition to love thy neighbor as thyself appears in the Old Testament.

10. In the case of adultery, the following people were to be put to death:
    a. the adulterer and the adulteress
    b. the adulterer
    c. the adulteress
    d. neither

11. True or False: Cursing one's father or mother carried the death penalty.

12. "In the year of this _____ ye shall return every man unto his possession." (Leviticus 25:13)

13. True or False: The fields were to have a year of rest every seventh year.

14. The priests were the sons of:
    a. Aaron   c. Lot
    b. Noah   d. Moses

15. True or False: After a victorious battle, it was permissible to take a female captive as a wife.

16. A rebellious son was to be punished by:
    a. stoning
    b. sacrificing a perfect ram
    c. hanging
    d. humbling himself to his father

17. "Thou shalt not remove thy neighbour's
    _____, which they of old time
    have set in thine inheritance, which thou
    shalt inherit in the land that the LORD
    thy God giveth thee to possess it."

18. How many witnesses were required to
    put someone to death for committing a
    crime?

19. True or False: The Israelites were
    instructed not to let a witch live.

20. Leprosy was diagnosed by:
    a. doctors   c. magicians
    b. priests   d. other lepers

21. True or False: Provisions for handling
    garments infected with leprosy appear in
    Leviticus.

22. The person who ate blood could expect:
    a. a stomachache
    b. to be stoned
    c. the Lord's face to be set against his soul and to be cut off from his people
    d. to be hanged

23. True or False: The Israelites were given the right to avenge those who wronged them.

24. If a poverty-stricken brother sold himself to a man, he was to be considered:
    a. an indentured servant
    b. forgiven
    c. a hired servant
    d. a slave

25. "Thou shalt have no other _____ before me."

ECCLESIASTES

1. The Book of Ecclesiastes is located directly after:
   a. Deuteronomy
   b. Psalms
   c. Jude
   d. Proverbs

2. Who wrote Ecclesiastes?

3. What is the theme of Ecclesiastes?

4. True or False: Ecclesiastes focuses on wisdom rather than history.

5. Ecclesiastes proclaims that all is:
   a. God's
   b. blessed
   c. vanity
   d. good

6. "I the _____ was king over Israel in Jerusalem."

7. True or False: Solomon proclaims that there is much that is new under the sun.

8. A fool's voice is known by its:
   a. few words
   b. high pitch
   c. faulty grammar
   d. multitude of words

14

9. Solomon hated his labor because:
   a. his 401k went south when the stock market crashed in 931 B.C.
   b. his concubines demanded silver
   c. he didn't like to sweat under the sun
   d. his money would go to his heirs, and he didn't know if they would be fools

10. "To every thing there is a _____, and a time to every purpose under the heaven."

11. Solomon names twenty-eight events that have a time. Can you name all of them?

12. The following rock song includes portions of Ecclesiastes 3:1–8:
    a. "Turn, Turn, Turn" by the Byrds
    b. "Money" by Pink Floyd
    c. "Round and Round" by Aerosmith
    d. "Hotel California" by the Eagles

13. "Moreover the profit of the earth is for all: the _____ himself is served by the field."

14. True or False: Solomon says that it is God's gift to enjoy the fruits of one's labor.

15. "A good _____ is better than precious ointment."

16. True or False: Ecclesiastes says that sorrow is better than laughter.

17. Anger rests in:
    a. the shrewish wife   c. the oppressed
    b. the bosom of fools   d. the righteous

18. True or False: Solomon longed for the good old days of the past, when times were simpler and men were wiser.

19. True or False: Solomon advises consulting the dead, as they possess the wisdom of the ages.

20. Perfume is fouled by:
    a. muddy water   c. inferior alcohol
    b. dead flies   d. age

21. What does Solomon mean by the above comparison?

22. We should remember Whom in the days of our youth?

23. "Therefore remove sorrow from thy
    heart, and put away evil from thy flesh:
    for childhood and youth are _____."

24. The words of the wise are as:
    a. roses   c. goads
    b. pearls   d. love

25. What is the whole duty of man?

1 Samuel Rivals

1. Who was Hannah's rival?

2. After Hannah gave birth to Samuel, she bore:
   a. no other children
   b. three sons and two daughters
   c. two sons and three daughters
   d. the world's first set of quintuplets

3. The Lord called Samuel three times because:
   a. Samuel was born partially deaf
   b. he wanted to stress to Samuel the importance of the Holy Trinity
   c. Samuel was too preoccupied studying the Torah to hear the Lord
   d. Samuel did not yet know the Lord

4. What did the Lord tell Samuel about Eli's house?

5. True or False: Samuel did not tell Eli everything the Lord revealed to him.

6. True or False: The new judges were upright and fair.

7. For how many months did the ark of the Lord stay in the land of the Philistines?

8. True or False: The Philistines were blessed with prosperity while the ark of the Lord was in their possession.

9. Samuel appointed as his successors:
   a. his sons
   b. his daughters, because he had no sons
   c. rabbis he deemed particularly studious
   d. Aaron and his sons

10. Dagon was:
    a. the god of Icabod
    b. a god of Egypt
    c. a god of the Philistines
    d. Dagwood's brother

11. After the new judges took office, the Israelites asked Samuel for:
    a. a festival to honor the judges
    b. a king to rule over them instead of judges
    c. a prayer to God that judges would always rule over them
    d. a democracy

12. Identify the person who said the following: "And now, behold, the king walketh before you: and I am old and grayheaded; and, behold, my sons are with you: and I have walked before you from my childhood unto this day."

13. Saul reigned for _____ years.

14. The following person could not be found in Israel:
    a. priest   c. horse trader
    b. jeweler   d. blacksmith

15. Where was Saul when Jonathan asked his armor-bearer to go with him to the Philistines' garrison?

16. Jonathan violated his father's oath against his enemies because he:
    a. wanted to rebel against his father
    b. had not heard the oath
    c. loved David more than Saul
    d. was hungry

17. True or False: David tried to convince Achish the king of Gath that he was insane.

18. "And there went out a champion out of the camp of the Philistines, named _____, of Gath, whose height was six cubits and a span."

19. Why did the women's song ignite Saul's resentment against David?

20. True or False: The Bible describes David as homely in countenance.

21. As he spared Saul's life, David cut:
    a. the end of Saul's sash
    b. Saul's ear
    c. the corner of Saul's robe
    d. a lock of Saul's hair

22. True or False: Samuel was buried in Ramah.

23. "Now the name of the man was Nabal; and the name of his wife _____: and she was a woman of good understanding, and of a beautiful countenance: but the man was churlish and evil in his doings; and he was of the house of Caleb."

24. True or False: Nabal of Maon was a rich man who possessed an abundance of sheep and goats.

25. Whom did Nabal's wife marry after Nabal died?

WHERE WAS THAT?

1. In what garden was Eve tempted by Satan?

2. After God drove Adam and Eve out of the garden, He placed cherubim:
   a. at the east of the garden
   b. on the path leading to the Tree of Life
   c. around his throne
   d. on their shoulders

3. On what mountain did Noah's ark come to rest?

4. True or False: The Law was given to Moses on Mount Sinai.

5. Jesus told His disciples about the end of the age as He sat:
   a. in the Garden of Gethsemane
   b. on the Mount of Olives
   c. on Mount Sinai
   d. on Mount Hermon

6. True or False: King Ahasuerus ruled over 127 provinces extending from India to Ethiopia.

7. In what river did John the Baptist baptize those who repented?

8. In what room was The Lord's Supper instituted?

9. After Lot chose to dwell on the plain of Jordan, Abram went to:
   a. Egypt   c. Mount Ararat
   b. Sodom   d. Canaan

10. True or False: Abraham's wife Sarah was buried in Canaan.

11. Upon God's instruction, Moses struck a rock to gain drinking water for the Israelites. The rock was located in:
    a. Egypt   c. Canaan
    b. Samaria   d. Horeb

12. True or False: God instructed Moses to send spies into Canaan.

13. Job lived in:
    a. Babylon   c. Egypt
    b. Canaan   d. Uz

14. "And when they were departed, behold, the angel of the Lord appeareth to Joseph in a dream, saying, Arise, and take the young child and his mother, and flee into _____, and be thou there until I bring thee word: for Herod will seek the young child to destroy him."

15. On what island was John when he received The Revelation from Jesus?

16. True or False: The seven churches addressed in The Revelation were located in Asia Minor.

17. When Jesus returned to His hometown of Nazareth, He was:
    a. crucified
    b. rejected
    c. greeted with resounding cheers
    d. asked to heal ten lepers

18. Why did Jesus leave Galilee even though the Galileans knew He was the Messiah?

19. Paul found an altar with the inscription TO THE UNKNOWN GOD in what Greek city?

20. After Jesus' birth, jealous King Herod had all the infant males killed in:
    a. Egypt
    b. Sodom and its districts
    c. Bethlehem
    d. Bethlehem and its districts

21. To what city did God tell Jonah to go?

22. Instead of going to the city God told him, Jonah went to:
    a. Joppa   c. Tarshish
    b. Ninevah   d. Jerusalem

23. During his journey, Jonah traveled:
    a. with a merchant caravan
    b. on a ship
    c. on a borrowed donkey
    d. with his brothers

24. How long did Jonah stay inside the fish?

25. "Where is he that is born King of the Jews? for we have seen his star in the _____, and are come to worship him."

ONE SMOOTH TALKER

1. True or False: The seventh chapter of Proverbs is told from the perspective of the young man who is the target of a seductive harlot.

2. According to Proverbs 7, whose house is the way to hell?

3. Who is the sister that will keep a man away from the harlot?

4. The kinswoman who will help a man stay away from the harlot is:
   a. chastity
   b. his mother
   c. the wife of his youth
   d. understanding

5. True or False: Though she later became bold in her seduction, the harlot was at first shy and reticent.

6. The harlot felt free to act brazenly because:
   a. her husband was out of town
   b. she was not married
   c. her male relatives had died in battle, so she answered to no one
   d. she was a sojourner

7. The harlot is described as:
   a. beautiful in countenance, but evil within
   b. comely
   c. poverty-stricken
   d. loud and stubborn

8. How did the harlot describe the decorations on her bed?

9. The harlot had perfumed her bed with:
   a. rose petals
   b. ointment from Egypt
   c. costly perfume from Damascus
   d. myrrh, aloes, and cinnamon

10. What did the harlot say was to be their solace?

11. True or False: The young man succumbed to her seduction.

12. The young man is compared to:
   a. an ox, a fool, and a bird
   b. a lamb, a fool, and a virgin
   c. an ox, a dullard, and a ram
   d. a blistering sore, a frog, and a fly

13. True or False: The harlot has slain many strong men.

14. Where does the harlot lie in wait for all of us?

15. Why do you think Solomon devotes an entire chapter of Proverbs to a scene of seduction?

AN ABUNDANCE OF LIVING CREATURES

1. Why would the Lord enjoy a burnt or baked offering?

2. "That thy foot may be dipped in the blood of thine enemies, and the tongue of thy _____ in the same."

3. True or False: God instructed Adam and Eve to subdue the earth.

4. True or False: It is permissible under Mosaic law for an Israelite to eat an oyster.

5. "Then said Jesus unto them again, 'Verily, verily, I say unto you, I am the door of the _____.'"

6. A wave offering represented:
   a. sanctification   c. consecration
   b. confirmation   d. deification

7. True or False: The King James Bible mentions unicorns.

8. What color was the dragon defeated by Michael and his angels in the heavenly war?

9. Job's donkeys and oxen were stolen by the:
   a. Chaldeans   c. Sabeans
   b. Amorites   d. Samaritans

10. Jesus instructed His disciples to loosen a colt before His triumphant entry. What were they to say to anyone who questioned them?

11. "His head is as the most fine gold, his locks are bushy, and black as a _____."

12. True or False: During the plagues, the Israelites' livestock was spared while the Egyptians' was stricken with sickness.

13. What animal's mouth did David pray to be saved from?

14. True or False: Under Mosaic law, the Israelites were allowed to eat locusts, beetles, and grasshoppers.

15. On which day did God create the great sea creatures?

16. Job's camels were taken by:
    a. Chaldeans   c. Sabeans
    b. Amorites   d. Samaritans

17. "I am the good shepherd, and know my _____, and am known of mine."

18. To whom does the following verse refer? "But these, as natural brute beasts, made to be taken and destroyed, speak evil of the things that they understand not; and shall utterly perish in their own corruption."

19. True or False: Job's sheep were stricken with disease.

20. What part of an animal's flesh belongs to the Lord?

21. The three unclean spirits that John saw come out of the mouth of the dragon, the beast, and the false prophet were like:
    a. locusts   c. flies
    b. frogs   d. gnats

22. "There is a lad here, which hath five barley loaves, and _____ small fishes: but what are they among so many?"

23. God rid Egypt of the locust plague by sending:
    a. worms to eat them
    b. a flood of the Nile River to swallow them
    c. a strong wind to sweep them away
    d. birds to devour them

24. "And said unto them that sold _____, 'Take these things hence; make not my Father's house an house of merchandise.'"

25. How does the first chapter of Genesis describe God's creation after the sixth day?

THE WICKED

1. "Give not that which is holy unto the dogs, neither cast ye your pearls before _____, lest they trample them under their feet, and turn again and rend you."

2. Why should we not fret about or be envious of the wicked?

3. The wicked are like a garment that shall be eaten by:
   a. age   c. fleas
   b. maggots   d. moths

4. True or False: Silver and gold can deliver the wicked in the day of the Lord's wrath.

5. "For every tree is known by his own _____."

6. The Pharisees criticized Jesus for befriending:
   a. publicans and sinners
   b. lowly fisherman and shepherds
   c. Gentiles
   d. Samaritans

7. True or False: David compared his enemies to a greedy lion.

8. "These are wells without _____, clouds that are carried with a tempest; to whom the mist of darkness is reserved for ever."

9. Before ministering to Jesus, Mary called Magdalene had been purged of:
   a. leprosy   c. lameness
   b. seven devils   d. blindness

10. "That the triumphing of the wicked is short, and the joy of the _____ but for a moment?"

11. The man whose heart departs from God shall be like a:
    a. dog without food
    b. tax collector
    c. heath in the desert
    d. computer without a monitor

12. True or False: God warned Ezekiel that the Israelites were rebellious.

13. To whom did God send seven plagues?

14. What did Jesus mean when He compared the scribes and Pharisees to whited sepulchres?

15. After God warned Joseph that the baby Jesus was in danger, Joseph took his family to:
   a. Gilead   c. Bethlehem
   b. Jerusalem   d. Egypt

16. What prophet did Balak ask to curse Israel?

17. According to Proverbs, a flattering mouth worketh:
   a. trust   c. ruin
   b. greed   d. envy

18. What is the unpardonable sin?

19. Who tried to kill the baby Jesus?

20. True or False: Haman was hanged on the gallows that he had built for Mordecai.

21. Jesus sent the demon Legion into a herd of:
   a. swine   c. sheep
   b. goats   d. cows

22. "He that is without sin among you, let him first cast a _____ at her."

23. True or False: A multitude attempted to stone Paul to death.

24. If you give your enemy food and drink you will be:
    a. burning bridges behind you
    b. heaping coals of fire upon his head
    c. sending smoke signals
    d. adding fuel to the fire

25. True or False: According to Jude, there are no apostates in the church.

GENESIS

1. Who was tricked into marrying Leah after working seven years to marry her sister Rachel?

2. True or False: Abraham remarried after Sarah's death.

3. The boy whose father made him a tunic of many colors was:
   a. Jacob   c. Joseph
   b. Abraham   d. Moses

4. "And _____ went in, and his sons, and his wife, and his sons' wives with him, into the ark, because of the waters of the flood."

5. True or False: Abraham sent a servant to his native land to find a wife for Isaac.

6. "Neither shall thy name any more be called Abram, but thy name shall be _____; for a father of many nations have I made thee."

7. The one who pleaded with God to spare Sodom for the sake of ten righteous men was:
   a. Lot   c. Moses
   b. Abraham   d. Noah

8. Which of Joseph's brothers convinced the other brothers to throw Joseph in a pit rather than to kill him?

9. True or False: Lot and his two daughters dwelt in a cave after their city was destroyed.

10. Joseph was accused of pursuing Potiphar's wife by:
    a. Pharaoh
    b. Potiphar's wife
    c. his brother Benjamin
    d. Joseph's rival

11. "Therefore is the name of it called _____; because the LORD did there confound the language of all the earth: and from thence did the LORD scatter them abroad upon the face of all the earth."

12. Jacob lied to his father to rob his brother
    Esau of his:
    a. birthright   c. firstborn son
    b. wife   d. blessing

13. True or False: God told Noah and his
    sons to be fruitful and to multiply.

14. What land did Lot choose for himself
    when he and Abram separated?

15. Among the wicked inhabiting the earth,
    the one man who found grace in the eyes
    of the Lord was:
    a. Noah   c. Methuselah
    b. Enosh   d. Adam

16. According to Genesis 5:24, Enoch "was
    not; for God took him." What does this
    mean?

17. "And the LORD God planted a garden
    eastward in _____; and there he put
    the man whom he had formed."

18. True or False: Isaac told the men of
    Gerar that Rebekah was his wife.

19. How many rivers does Genesis say ran through Eden?

20. Who dreamed that there would be plenty in Egypt, followed by famine?

21. The dreams of feast and famine for Egypt pictured:
    a. cows and corn   c. sheep and corn
    b. frogs and wheat   d. cows and rye

22. "And they came to the place which God had told him of; and Abraham built an altar there, and laid the wood in order, and bound _____ his son, and laid him on the altar upon the wood."

23. How did God keep the people from completing the Tower of Babel?

24. Esau sold his birthright to Jacob for:
    a. thirty talents of silver
    b. a coat of many colors
    c. a bowl of stew and some bread
    d. a bowl of stew

25. True or False: The last event recorded in Genesis is Jacob's death.

MAMMON

1. "For where your treasure is, there will your _____ be also."

2. What happens to earthly treasures?

3. A man cannot serve two masters because:
   a. he will hate one and love the other
   b. one will treat him better than the other will
   c. one will pay a better salary than the other
   d. he will have to work from sunup to sundown to serve both

4. True or False: The beggar Lazarus visited the rich man's five brothers to warn them that they would be tormented if they did not feed the poor.

5. The beggar Lazarus asked the rich man for:
   a. a job in his vineyard
   b. salve for his sores
   c. water to bathe his dusty feet
   d. crumbs from his table

6. The rich man asked Lazarus for:
   a. a drop of water to relieve his torment from the flames of hell
   b. crumbs from his table in heaven
   c. a prayer for him
   d. a new pitchfork

7. How much money did the poor widow give to the treasury?

8. According to Proverbs, strangers will be filled with the wealth of a man who succumbs to:
   a. the love of money   c. idleness
   b. a strange woman   d. greed

9. True or False: The precedent of tithing one-tenth of one's goods is set forth in Genesis.

10. Under Mosaic law, those who took their neighbors' garments in pledge were required to return them:
    a. during the year of Jubilee
    b. on the Sabbath
    c. by sundown
    d. after the debt was paid

11. What did Jesus have to say about paying taxes?

12. True or False: The virtuous woman described in Proverbs cares for the needy.

13. When you lend, hope:
    a. to be repaid quickly, with interest
    b. for nothing again
    c. that the borrower will not be filing for bankruptcy any time soon
    d. to be repaid quickly, but you are not to charge interest

14. True or False: The disciples were pleased with the woman who anointed Jesus with precious ointment contained in a costly alabaster box.

15. Who tried to buy the gift of God?

16. The woman who has ten coins and loses one:
    a. shrugs her shoulders
    b. searches until she finds it
    c. doesn't tithe the following Sabbath
    d. moans with grief

17. "Ye cannot serve God and _____."

18. Why was the rich young ruler sorrowful when Jesus told him to sell what he had and give the proceeds to the poor?

19. True or False: Job's wealth was restored after he remained faithful to God during his temptation from Satan.

20. Judas agreed to betray Jesus in exchange for:
    a. thirty pieces of silver
    b. the favor of a comely woman
    c. high political office
    d. a portion of the Israelites' wave-offerings

21. What happens to the wealth of a man who keeps company with prostitutes?

22. True or False: The fabulously rich King Solomon proclaimed that silver satisfies the soul.

23. Who grants the power to gain wealth?

24. "Labour not to be _____: cease from thine own wisdom."

25. True or False: According to 1 Timothy, money is the root of all evil.

JOY

1. True or False: Joy is a fruit of the spirit.

2. Why did the rich farmer build bigger barns for his goods?

3. "But godliness with _____ is great gain."

4. In whom does Timothy say the rich should put their trust?

5. "Bring ye all the _____ into the storehouse, that there may be meat in mine house, and prove me now herewith, saith the Lord of hosts, if I will not open you the windows of heaven, and pour you out a blessing, that there shall not be room enough to receive it."

6. True or False: According to Proverbs, a woman's greatest joy lies in her beauty.

7. "Be not deceived; God is not mocked: for whatsoever a man soweth, that shall he also _____."

8. "Whoso loveth instruction loveth knowledge: but he that hateth reproof is _____."
   a. wise   c. brutish
   b. angry   d. college-bound

9. "The light of the righteous _____: but the lamp of the wicked shall be put out."

10. True or False: Paul commended the Thessalonians for receiving God's Word with joy, becoming examples to other Christians.

11. "Every man according as he purposeth in his heart, so let him give; not grudgingly, or of necessity: for God loveth a _____ giver."

12. Jesus told His disciples that it is easier for a camel to go through the eye of a needle than for a rich man to enter into the kingdom of God. After He made that observation, what words of comfort did He then offer His astonished disciples?

13. True or False. The servant who hid his lord's treasure to preserve it was heartily rewarded.

14. "I have shewed you all things, how that so labouring ye ought to support the weak, and to remember the words of the Lord Jesus, how he said, 'It is more blessed to _____ than to receive.'"

15. Solomon in all his glory was not arrayed as beautifully as:
    a. the lilies of the field
    b. the trees in the valley
    c. the daisies of the wild
    d. locusts and wild honey

16. Though King Solomon was rich beyond compare during his lifetime, in Ecclesiastes he says the greatest asset is:
    a. wisdom
    b. a comely countenance
    c. many heirs
    d. the wife of your youth

17. The Song of Solomon is his tribute to his:
    a. wealth
    b. favorite musical group, *The Four Flutists*
    c. children
    d. bride

18. "Who can find a virtuous woman? for her price is far above _____."

19. The Proverbs woman wears:
    a. a little black dress   c. white
    b. orange   d. purple

20. What beareth all things, believeth all things, hopeth all things, endureth all things?

21. According to Psalm 100:2, the Lord should be served with:
    a. honor   c. honesty
    b. duty   d. gladness

22. True or False: Philip healed many in Samaria after preaching Christ to them, and there was great joy in that city.

23. "His lord said unto him, 'Well done, good and faithful _____.' "

24. The joy of the hypocrite is:
    a. great   c. everlasting
    b. resounding   d. short-lived

25. True or False: There is more joy in heaven over one sinner who repents than over ninety-nine just persons who need no repentance.

STORIES JESUS TOLD

1. The book of the Bible containing the greatest number of parables is:
   a. Matthew
   b. Mark
   c. Luke
   d. John

2. What three types of ground are mentioned in the parable of the sower?

3. True or False: People who have no root in the Word will rejoice in it until they are persecuted.

4. A wise man builds his house on:
   a. sand
   b. rock
   c. soil
   d. prime real estate

5. "The sower soweth the _____."

6. The parable of the sower compares thorns to:
   a. swords
   b. worldly cares, riches, and lusts
   c. strangling ropes
   d. prickly pins

7. Jesus said, "Heaven and earth shall pass away: but my _____ shall not pass away."

8. What did Jesus mean by comparing the kingdom of heaven to a fishing net?

9. True or False: The unjust judge avenged the widow because he felt a surge of compassion for her plight.

10. How many sinners' repentance does it take to cause great joy in the presence of the angels of God?

11. When his younger brother returned home after squandering his inheritance, the faithful older brother:
    a. killed the fatted calf
    b. threw a party for his brother
    c. protested angrily to his father for celebrating
    d. convinced his father to cut him off from the family forever

12. The prodigal son asked his father for:
    a. a trust fund for his heirs
    b. a hefty stock portfolio
    c. a job as a hired servant
    d. permission to marry

13. "Salt is good: but if the salt have lost his _____, wherewith shall it be seasoned?"

14. "And the Pharisees and scribes murmured, saying, This man receiveth sinners, and eateth with them." Who is the man?

15. The parable of the ten virgins warns us to be:
    a. thrifty with oil
    b. watchful for the Son of Man
    c. prepared to make quick purchases
    d. merciful to the foolish

16. To what type of seed is the kingdom of heaven compared?

17. Why should we not seek friends, brothers, or the rich as dinner guests, but the poor, maimed, lame, and blind?

18. "If thy whole _____ therefore be full of light, having no part dark, the whole shall be full of light, as when the bright shining of a candle doth give thee light."

19. Luke records three parables of the lost. They are the lost:
    a. sheep, pearl, and son
    b. ram, coin, and son
    c. sheep, coin, and wife
    d. sheep, coin, and son

20. True or False: The parable of the prodigal son appears in the Gospels of Matthew, Mark, and Luke.

21. Who planted tares in the man's wheat field as he slept?

22. The man wouldn't let his servants pull the tares from the wheat until after the wheat was harvested because:
    a. the tares helped to fertilize the soil
    b. the wheat could be uprooted along with the tares
    c. he could write off the crop damage on his taxes
    d. the tares would do little damage to the wheat

23. Why was the tax collector, a confessed sinner, greater in God's eyes than the prayerful Pharisee?

24. Who is the son in the parable of the vineyard owner?

25. True or False: Most of Jesus' parables are recorded in John's Gospel.

A Message to the Churches

1. Where is The Revelation located in the Bible?

2. The Revelation was witnessed by:
   a. Jesus
   b. John
   c. Paul
   d. Adam

3. Who revealed The Revelation?

4. True or False: The Revelation came from God.

5. According to The Revelation's introduction, those who read and hear the words of The Revelation will be:
   a. saved
   b. blessed
   c. all-knowing
   d. frightened

6. How many churches did The Revelation address?

7. Which church bore the same name as the City of Brotherly Love?

8. Can you name all the churches addressed in The Revelation?

9. The churches were located in:
   a. China   c. Asia Minor
   b. Sodom   d. Iraq

10. True or False: Jesus is not quoted in the book of The Revelation.

11. " 'I am _____ and Omega, the beginning and the ending,' saith the Lord, 'which is, and which was, and which is to come, the Almighty.' "

12. True or False: Jesus commended all of the churches.

13. The church of Ephesus had left its:
    a. offerings unprotected
    b. first love
    c. poor to suffer needlessly
    d. compassion at the front door

14. Jesus commends the church of Ephesus for:
    a. tireless labor for Him
    b. chastity
    c. good music
    d. faithful tithing

15. What was predicted for the church in Smyrna?

16. Jesus said to the church at Smyrna, "be thou faithful unto death, and I will give thee a crown of _____."

17. The church in Thyatira was:
    a. sexually immoral
    b. running a lottery
    c. pocketing the local tax on wine
    d. selling doves for sacrifices on the church steps

18. True or False: The Thyatira prophetess Jezebel repented after Jesus gave her more time to do so.

19. Who in the church in Sardis was already worthy of Jesus?

20. True or False: One of the offenses of the church in Pergamos was holding to false doctrine.

21. Jesus promised the church in Philadelphia:
    a. a visit from Jezebel
    b. that they would be delivered from the hour of temptation
    c. their agape love for each other would increase
    d. a city would be named after them

22. "So then because thou art _____, and neither cold nor hot, I will spue thee out of my mouth."

23. The Laodiceans thought they needed nothing because they possessed wealth. In fact, Jesus said they were:
    a. blessed
    b. in keeping with the rule to tithe 10% of their incomes to the church
    c. as wise as Solomon himself
    d. wretched, and miserable, and poor, and blind, and naked

24. Jesus tells the unrighteous they must:
    a. repent
    b. donate more money to the poor
    c. honor the governor
    d. read more Scripture

25. Whom among all of us does Jesus chasten and rebuke?

A NEW CHRISTIAN
BEGINS HIS MINISTRY

1. True or False: The Book of Acts is Paul's firsthand account of events that took place in the early days of the church.

2. What was Paul called before he became a Christian?

3. True or False: Saul was present at the stoning of Stephen.

4. Saul was converted on the road to Damascus. Why was he going there?

5. What did Jesus first say to Saul?

6. True or False: At first, Saul resisted Jesus' commands.

7. Saul was staying at Judas's house on the street in Damascus called:
   a. Crooked
   b. Easy
   c. The Great White Way
   d. Straight

8. What else did Jesus tell Ananias He would show Saul?

9. Jesus told Ananias in a vision that Saul was His chosen vessel to:
   a. carry His name to more Jews
   b. be an example of how the rich should live righteously
   c. write more epistles than any other apostle
   d. bear His name to the Gentiles, the kings, and the children of Israel

10. True or False: Saul was blind for three days after seeing Jesus in a vision on the road to Damascus.

11. Who was Ananias?

12. Saul found Damascus by:
    a. following a cloud
    b. following a star
    c. following the sound of Jesus' voice
    d. being led by the hands of his traveling companions

13. After Saul was baptized and had been strengthened, the Bible says, "And straightway he preached Christ in the synagogues, that he is the Son of _____."

14. All who heard Saul preach were:
    a. disgusted   c. baptized
    b. annoyed   d. amazed

15. The Greeks responded to Saul's bold preaching by:
    a. planning to slay him
    b. converting to Christianity
    c. smashing their idols on the temple floor
    d. chasing him out of the country

16. At what point does the Bible begin to refer to Saul as Paul?

17. True or False: Paul carried out his intent to minister to Asia Minor, which is modern Turkey.

18. After passing through Asia Minor, Silas and Paul went to:
    a. Macedonia   c. Greece
    b. Troas   d. Iraq

19. Paul and Silas were asked to go to Macedonia by:
    a. a vision of a Macedonian man
    b. a vision of Jesus
    c. Peter
    d. Martha and Mary

20. What did the Macedonian fortune-teller, possessed by a spirit of divination, say about Paul and Silas?

21. How long did she say this?

22. "But Paul, being grieved, turned and said to the spirit, 'I command thee in the name of _____ _____ to come out of her.' And he came out the same hour."

23. When the fortune-teller's masters heard that Paul had rid the girl of the spirit of divination, they were eager to:
    a. be baptized
    b. have him imprisoned
    c. invite them to their home
    d. be cured of their own spirit possession

24. What charges did the fortune-teller's masters levy against Paul and the other missionaries with him?

25. True or False: Paul and Silas griped and complained as they stayed in the Macedonian prison.

26. God set them free by:
    a. giving the jailer a soft heart, so that he loosened their bands
    b. smiting their accusers so not one was left alive in the city
    c. sending an earthquake that loosened their bands
    d. afflicting the populace with boils until they begged them to leave

27. Afraid that the prisoners had fled, the jailer:
    a. drew a sign saying "Wanted: Dead or Alive"
    b. vowed to find them
    c. drew his sword to kill himself
    d. wept

28. True or False: The prisoners had fled.

29. What did the jailer ask Paul and Silas after they were freed?

30. "And they said, Believe on the Lord Jesus Christ, and thou shalt be _____, and thy house."

MIRACLES

1. True or False: The Bible says that Jonah was swallowed by a whale.

2. How many baskets of food were left over after Jesus fed the five thousand from five loaves of bread and two fishes?

3. True or False: Jesus healed a man even at the moment of His betrayal by Judas.

4. When Jesus performed the miracle of helping the fishermen catch two full boatloads of fish, Simon Peter:
   a. asked Jesus to leave him
   b. told Jesus he was a rabbi who had studied to be His disciple
   c. promised to increase his tithe to the temple
   d. said he would give all the fish to the poor

5. "But God prepared a _____ when the morning rose the next day, and it smote the gourd that it withered."

6. After Christ cleansed ten lepers, how many thanked Him?

7. To show Jonah he should have pity on Ninevah, God first caused Jonah to pity a:
   a. little boy   c. group of sailors
   b. big fish   d. gourd

8. What did Jesus do for Simon Peter and his partners after an unsuccessful fishing expedition?

9. How many days had Lazarus been dead before Jesus brought him back to life?

10. "And the Lord said, 'If ye had _____ as a grain of mustard seed, ye might say unto this sycamine tree, Be thou plucked up by the root, and be thou planted in the sea; and it should obey you.'"

11. Moses asked God to help him provide water for the Israelites because he:
    a. was tired of not getting enough credit for his heroic deeds
    b. wanted to show he was superior to his brother Aaron
    c. was as thirsty as they were
    d. was afraid they would stone him

12. Where was Jesus' first miracle performed?

13. True or False: Sorcerers in Pharaoh's court were unable to duplicate the miracle of Aaron's rod turning into a serpent.

14. After all the rods were thrown to the ground, Aaron's rod:
    a. disappeared
    b. turned into gold
    c. ate the other rods
    d. etched a message on Pharaoh's floor

15. True or False: The plagues God sent to Egypt were aimed to refute the worthiness of specific Egyptian deities.

16. What was the final plague that convinced Pharaoh to beg the Israelites to leave Egypt?

17. "And the _____ shall be to you for a token upon the houses where ye are: and when I see the _____, I will pass over you, and the plague shall not be upon you to destroy you, when I smite the land of Egypt."

18. The memorial instituted by God's sparing the Israelites' children during the last plague of Egypt is called:
    a. Hanukkah
    b. Rosh Hashanah
    c. Yom Kippur
    d. Passover

19. Which disciple doubted Jesus' resurrection?

20. "Jesus saith unto him, 'Thomas, because thou hast seen me, thou hast _____: blessed are they that have not seen, and yet have _____.' "

21. When Mary saw the risen Christ, at first she thought He was:
    a. the gardener
    b. the funeral director
    c. a hallucination
    d. an angel

22. Who saw the handwriting on the wall?

23. True or False: King Belshazzar offended God by throwing a wild party for his lords.

24. After God delivered Daniel from the lion's den, King Darius decreed that:
    a. a holiday was to be established in Daniel's honor
    b. Daniel was to be hanged instead
    c. Daniel's God is the living God
    d. a statue in Daniel's likeness was to be erected in the town square

25. "Jesus said unto her, 'I am the resurrection, and the _____: he that believeth in me, though he were dead, yet shall he live.'"

ANSWER KEY

<u>PROVERBIAL PEARLS</u>

1. Solomon wrote most of this book (Proverbs 1:1), but King Lemuel's mother is credited with a portion of its wisdom. (Proverbs 31:1)
2. b. young man. (Proverbs 4:1)
3. LORD (Proverbs 1:7)
4. c. fools. (Proverbs 1:7)
5. prosperity (Proverbs 1:32)
6. "For the LORD giveth wisdom: out of his mouth cometh knowledge and understanding." (Proverbs 2:6)
7. a. death. (Proverbs 2:16–18)
8. LORD (Proverbs 3:5)
9. The Lord corrects those He loves. (Proverbs 3:11–12)
10. True. (Proverbs 3:15)
11. d. a tree of life. (Proverbs 3:18)
12. b. glory. (Proverbs 3:35)
13. True. (Proverbs 4:13)
14. b. ant. (Proverbs 6:6) Proverbs encourages the lazy to adopt the working ways of the busy ant.
15. cistern (Proverbs 5:15)
16. Be faithful to one's own wife, for the Lord notices adultery. (Proverbs 5:18–21)
17. The abominations named in Proverbs 6:16–19 are: a proud look, a lying tongue, hands that shed innocent blood, a heart that devises wicked imaginations, feet swift to seek mischief, a false witness that speaks

lies, and one who sows discord among
brethren.

18. evil (Proverbs 8:13)
19. True. (Proverbs 9:10–11)
20. True. (Proverbs 9:17). Even so, verse 18
    warns that forbidden pleasures lead to hell.
21. a. choice silver. (Proverbs 10:20)
22. False. "A false balance is abomination to the
    LORD." (Proverbs 11:1)
23. b. secrets. (Proverbs 11:13)
24. False. "Where no counsel is, the people fall:
    but in the multitude of counsellors there is
    safety." (Proverbs 11:14)
25. c. crown to her husband.
26. abomination (Proverbs 12:22)
27. "Wealth gotten by vanity shall be dimin-
    ished." (Proverbs 13:11)
28. rod (Proverbs 13:24)
29. "A soft answer turneth away wrath."
    (Proverbs 15:1)
30. Obviously, there is no right or wrong answer
    to this question. I hope you have enjoyed
    meditating upon the many pearls of wisdom
    in Proverbs.

IT'S THE LAW, SON

1. The Old Testament laws are found in the
   first five books of the Bible: Genesis,
   Exodus, Leviticus, Numbers, and
   Deuteronomy. They are concentrated in
   Leviticus and Deuteronomy.
2. Moses.

3. True. (Deuteronomy 24:5)
4. The penalty for kidnapping was death. (Deuteronomy 24:7)
5. holy (Exodus 20:8)
6. A baby boy was to be circumcised when he was eight days old. (Leviticus 12:3)
7. True. A woman was unclean for seven days after the birth of a boy, two weeks after the birth of a girl. (Leviticus 12:1–5)
8. God instructed people not to take everything from the harvest, but to leave some food in the fields for the poor to glean. (Leviticus 19:9–10)
9. True. (Leviticus 19:18)
10. a. the adulterer and the adulteress. (Leviticus 20:10)
11. True. (Leviticus 20:9)
12. jubile (Leviticus 25:13). The KJV says "year of this jubile" and the NKJV says "Year of Jubilee."
13. True. (Leviticus 25:3–5)
14. a. Aaron. (Leviticus 21:1)
15. True. (Deuteronomy 21:10–12) However, she was to be treated with compassion. The captive was allowed to mourn her parents for one month before the wedding, and she was to be freed if the husband found no delight in her. She was not to be sold for money. (Deuteronomy 13:14)
16. a. stoning. (Deuteronomy 21:18–21)
17. landmark (Deuteronomy 19:14)
18. Two or three witnesses were required to convict someone of a crime. The Bible

specifically states that the word of one person
alone could not make a conviction.
(Deuteronomy 17:6)

19. True. (Exodus 22:18) The KJV says "witch,"
while the NKJV says "sorceress."

20. b. priests. Leviticus 13:1–46 gives detailed
descriptions of the sores to help the priests
diagnose leprosy.

21. True. Leviticus 13:47–59 tells the priests how
to determine whether the leprosy is active and
how to dispose of infected clothing.

22. c. the Lord's face to be set against his
soul and to be cut off from his people.
(Leviticus 17:10)

23. False. (Leviticus 19:18)

24. c. a hired servant. (Leviticus 25:39–40)

25. gods (Exodus 20:3)

ECCLESIASTES

1. d. Proverbs.
2. Solomon wrote Ecclesiastes.
3. The theme of Ecclesiastes is to discourage
people from trying to find satisfaction from
earthly wealth and pleasures rather than from
the source of true satisfaction, God.
4. True. Although Solomon bases the wisdom
of Ecclesiastes on many of his personal
experiences, the book imparts wisdom to
future generations rather than focusing on
his life or his people's history.
5. c. vanity. (Ecclesiastes 1:2)
6. Preacher (Ecclesiastes 1:12)
7. False. Solomon tells us there is nothing new

under the sun. (Ecclesiastes 1:9)

8. d. multitude of words. (Ecclesiastes 5:3)

9. d. his money would go to his heirs, and he didn't know if they would be fools. (Ecclesiastes 2:18–19)

10. season (Ecclesiastes 3:1)

11. They are: born, die, plant, pluck up that which is planted, kill, heal, break down, build up, weep, laugh, mourn, dance, cast away stones, gather stones together, embrace, refrain from embracing, get, lose, keep, cast away, rend, sew, keep silence, speak, love, hate, war, peace. (Ecclesiastes 3:2–16)

12. a. "Turn, Turn, Turn" by the Byrds.

13. king (Ecclesiastes 5:9)

14. True. (Ecclesiastes 5:18–19)

15. name (Ecclesiastes 7:1)

16. True. Ecclesiastes 7:3 says, "Sorrow is better than laughter: for by the sadness of the countenance the heart is made better."

17. b. the bosom of fools (Ecclesiastes 7:9)

18. False. Solomon instructs us not to yearn for the past, for it is unwise to wonder if the past was better than the present day. (Ecclesiastes 7:10)

19. False. Solomon advises against consulting the dead. Instead, he says, "For the living know that they shall die: but the dead know not any thing, neither have they any more a reward; for the memory of them is forgotten." (Ecclesiastes 9:5)

20. b. dead flies. (Ecclesiastes 10:1)

21. The dead flies are to perfume as a small

amount of folly is to one who is considered
wise. (Ecclesiastes 10:1)
22. We should remember our Creator.
(Ecclesiastes 12:1)
23. vanity (Ecclesiastes 11:10)
24. c. goads. (Ecclesiastes 12:11)
25. The whole duty of man is to fear God
and to keep His commandments.
(Ecclesiastes 12:13)

1 SAMUEL RIVALS

1. Peninnah, her husband Elkanah's other wife.
(1 Samuel 1:2) Hannah was not able to bear
children, and Peninnah was. Peninnah never
let Hannah forget her barrenness. (1 Samuel
1:6) Still, Elkanah loved Hannah and
showed his love by giving Hannah more
than Peninnah. (1 Samuel 1:4–5)
2. b. three sons and two daughters. (1 Samuel
2:21). The Lord blessed Hannah with more
children after she kept her vow to devote her
firstborn to Him. (1 Samuel 1:27–28)
3. d. Samuel did not yet know the Lord.
(1 Samuel 3:7)
4. The Lord said He would judge Eli's house
because his sons were evil, and Eli did
nothing to stop their wickedness.
(1 Samuel 3:12–13)
5. False. 1 Samuel 3:18 says, "And Samuel told
him every whit, and hid nothing from him."
6. False. They took bribes and perverted judgment. (1 Samuel 8:3)
7. The ark of the Lord was in the country of

the Philistines for seven months.
(1 Samuel 6:1)

8. False. Rather than blessing, the ark brought nothing but sorrow to the Philistines. The Lord caused an image of their god Dagon to fall upon its face before the ark and to be destroyed. (1 Samuel 5:3–4) Then the Lord visited illness upon the Ashdodites. (1 Samuel 5:6) The Philistines passed the ark to the cities of Gath (v. 8) and Ekron (v. 10), who were similarly stricken. (1 Samuel 5:8–10). After that, they were begging to be rid of the ark. (1 Samuel 5:11–12)

9. a. his sons. (1 Samuel 8:1)

10. c. a god of the Philistines. (1 Samuel 5:2–5)

11. b. a king to rule over them instead of judges. (1 Samuel 8:6) They wanted to be like the other nations, ruled by a king. (1 Samuel 8:5)

12. Samuel. (1 Samuel 12:1–2)

13. 40 (Acts 13:21)

14. d. blacksmith. (1 Samuel 13:19)

15. He was sitting under a pomegranate tree in the outskirts of Gilbeah. (1 Samuel 14:2)

16. b. had not heard the oath. (1 Samuel 14:27)

17. True. (1 Samuel 21:13) David acted as a madman because he was afraid of the king. (1 Samuel 21:12)

18. Goliath (1 Samuel 17:4)

19. The song made Saul resentful because the women sang that David had slain ten thousands while Saul had only slain thousands. (1 Samuel 18:7)

20. False. He is described as ruddy, "withal of a

beautiful countenance, and goodly to look to." (1 Samuel 16:12)

21. c. the corner of Saul's robe. (1 Samuel 24:11) David did this to prove that although he had a chance to murder Saul, he did not. The action was meant to disprove the rumor that David was out to harm Saul. (1 Samuel 24:9–10)
22. True. (1 Samuel 25:1)
23. Abigail (1 Samuel 25:3)
24. True. (1 Samuel 25:2–3)
25. David. (1 Samuel 25:42)

WHERE WAS THAT?

1. Eden. Genesis 2:8 tells us the name of God's garden. Genesis 3:1–13 records Eve's temptation by Satan.
2. a. at the east of the garden. (Genesis 3:24)
3. Noah's ark came to rest on the mountains of Ararat. (Genesis 8:4)
4. True. (Exodus 19:20–25)
5. b. on the Mount of Olives. (Matthew 24:3)
6. True. (Esther 1:1) This verse, which helps set the scene for the Book of Esther, should give us a sense of the power Esther confronted as she revealed Haman's plot and thus saved the Jews.
7. John the Baptist baptized the repentant in the Jordan River. (Mark 1:5)
8. Jesus instituted The Lord's Supper in The Upper Room. (Luke 22:11–12)
9. d. Canaan. (Genesis 13:12)

10. True. (Genesis 23:19) Specifically, Sarah died in Kirjath-arba. (Genesis 23:2) Abraham paid four hundred shekels for a family burial place in Canaan, in the cave of the field of Machpelah. (Genesis 23) Although the plot was offered to Abraham gratis because of his high position, purchasing the land was important to Abraham because he was a for-eigner in Canaan. (Genesis 23:4)

11. d. Horeb. (Exodus 17:6)

12. True. (Numbers 13:1–2)

13. d. Uz. (Job 1:1)

14. Egypt (Matthew 2:13)

15. John was on the island of Patmos when he received The Revelation. (Revelation 1:9)

16. True. (Revelation 1:4) However, the KJV simply says they were in Asia.

17. b. rejected. (Luke 4:16–30)

18. Jesus told them He needed to preach to other cities. (Luke 4:40–44)

19. Paul found this altar in Athens. (Acts 17:22–24)

20. d. Bethlehem and its districts. (Matthew 2:16)

21. God instructed Jonah to go to Ninevah. (Jonah 1:2)

22. a. Joppa. (Jonah 1:3)

23. b. on a ship. (Jonah 1:3)

24. Jonah stayed in the fish for three days and three nights. (Jonah 1:17)

25. east (Matthew 2:2)

ONE SMOOTH TALKER

1. False. The perspective is that of the author watching the scene from a window. (Proverbs 7:6)

2. The harlot's house is the way to hell. (Proverbs 7:27)

3. The sister who will keep one away from the harlot is wisdom. (Proverbs 7:4)

4. d. understanding. (Proverbs 7:4)

5. False. The harlot was bold from the start. She was waiting for the young man, and when she spied him, she caught him, kissed him, and gave him an impudent look even before she began to speak. (Proverbs 7:13)

6. a. her husband was out of town. (Proverbs 7:19)

7. d. loud and stubborn. (Proverbs 7:11)

8. Her bed was decorated with fine linen from Egypt, tapestry, and carved works. (Proverbs 7:16)

9. d. myrrh, aloes, and cinnamon. (Proverbs 7:17)

10. Love was to be their solace. (Proverbs 7:18)

11. True. (Proverbs 7:22) Solomon describes him as "a young man void of understanding." (Proverbs 7:7)

12. a. Proverbs uses several comparisons to demonstrate the youth's folly. They are "as an ox goeth to the slaughter, or as a fool to the correction of the stocks." (Proverbs 7:22) Also, "as a bird hasteth to the snare, and knoweth not that it is for his life." (Proverbs 7:23)

13. True. (Proverbs 7:26)

14. The harlot, or temptation, lies in wait for us at every corner. (Proverbs 7:12)

15. Clearly, this incident is in keeping with a Proverbs theme that sexual fidelity is a hallmark of the wise. The young man allowed himself to be seduced by the harlot's flattery, which Solomon cautions against. His love of luxury added fuel to the fire, as the harlot was able to tempt him with fine decorations and sweet aromas. Solomon points out the young man's ignorance in allowing himself to be seduced by carnal pleasures, apparently unaware of the eternal consequences of his folly.

AN ABUNDANCE OF LIVING CREATURES

1. The aroma was sweet. (Leviticus 1:17)
2. dogs (Psalm 68:23)
3. True. (Genesis 1:28)
4. False. It violated God's law for an Israelite to eat a sea creature without fins or scales. (Leviticus 11:12)
5. sheep (John 10:7)
6. c. consecration. (Leviticus 8:29)
7. True. Job 39:10 is one reference, although unicorns are mentioned several times in the KJV. You might challenge yourself to find the other references. In Job 39:10, the NKJV translates "unicorn" as "wild ox."
8. Red. (Revelation 12:3)

9. c. Sabeans (Job 1:15)
10. "Because the Lord hath need of him." (Luke 19:31)
11. raven (Song of Solomon 5:11). This is part of a description of the bridegroom given by an adoring bride.
12. True. (Exodus 9:4)
13. Lion's. (Psalm 22:21)
14. True. (Leviticus 11:22)
15. The fifth day. (Genesis 1:21–23)
16. a. Chaldeans (Job 1:17)
17. sheep (John 10:14). Jesus is describing Himself as one who cares about those who are faithful to Him.
18. False teachers. (2 Peter 2:12)
19. False. They were destroyed by fire. (Job 1:16)
20. Its fat. (Leviticus 3:16)
21. b. frogs. (Revelation 16:13)
22. two (John 6:9). Jesus fed five thousand people with this portion of food that was the contents of a boy's lunch.
23. c. a strong wind to sweep them away. (Exodus 10:19)
24. doves (John 2:16)
25. "It was very good." (Genesis 1:31)

THE WICKED

1. swine (Matthew 7:6)
2. We should not envy the wicked because "they shall soon be cut down like the grass, and wither as the green herb." (Psalm 37:1–2)
3. d. moths. (Isaiah 51:8)

4. False. God cannot be bought with money. (Zephaniah 1:18)
5. fruit (Luke 6:44). With this parable Jesus cautioned against hypocrites, saying that no good tree produces bad fruit, and no bad tree produces good fruit. Likewise, what a man says reveals the good or the evil in his heart. (Luke 6:43–45)
6. a. publicans and sinners. (Luke 7:30 and 34) Publicans are also known as tax collectors.
7. True. (Psalm 17:12)
8. water (2 Peter 2:17)
9. b. seven devils. (Luke 8:2)
10. hypocrite (Job 20:5)
11. c. heath in the desert. (Jeremiah 17:5–6). The NKJV translates the word "heath" as "shrub."
12. True. (Ezekiel 2:4–5)
13. The Egyptians. (Exodus 6–12). God plagued the Egyptians with blood, frogs, insects, pestilence, boils, hail, and locusts.
14. Jesus was comparing the religious leaders of His day to hypocrites. Though they appeared pious to the casual observer, their hearts were evil. Specifically, "which indeed appear beautiful outward, but are within full of dead men's bones, and of all uncleanness. Even so ye also outwardly appear righteous unto men, but within ye are full of hypocrisy and iniquity." (Matthew 23:27–28)
15. d. Egypt. (Matthew 2:13–14)
16. Balaam. (Numbers 22:2–6)
17. c. ruin. (Proverbs 26:28)

18. The unpardonable sin is blasphemy against the Holy Spirit. (Matthew 12:31–32) Jesus rebuked the Pharisees who said Jesus' ability to heal was from Satan, not God. (Matthew 12:22–32)

19. Herod. (Matthew 2:16) The king felt threatened by this new baby the wise men worshiped. (Matthew 2:1–4)

20. True. (Esther 7:10)

21. a. swine. (Luke 8:30–33)

22. stone (John 8:7). John is the only Gospel writer to record Jesus' forgiveness of this adulteress.

23. True. (Acts 14:19–20) Though they left him for dead, Paul lived and escaped to Derbe with Barnabas.

24. b. heaping coals of fire upon his head. (Romans 12:20)

25. False. "For there are certain men crept in unawares, who were before of old ordained to this condemnation, ungodly men, turning the grace of our God into lasciviousness, and denying the only Lord God, and our Lord Jesus Christ." (Jude 4)

GENESIS

1. Jacob was tricked. (Genesis 29:18–28) Laban objected to giving his younger daughter, Rachel, in marriage before the elder, Leah. Jacob's love for Rachel led to much rivalry between the two sisters.

2. True. (Genesis 25:1–2) According to

Genesis, Keturah bore Abraham six children.

3. c. Joseph. (Genesis 37:3)
4. Noah (Genesis 7:7)
5. True. (Genesis 24:4)
6. Abraham (Genesis 17:5)
7. b. Abraham. (Genesis 18:23–33)
8. Reuben. (Genesis 37:21–22)
9. True. (Genesis 19:30)
10. b. Potiphar's wife. (Genesis 39:13–19) When Joseph spurned her advances, Potiphar's wife vengefully accused the young Hebrew of pursuing her. As a result, Joseph was thrown into prison, where God's plan for him began to unfold.
11. Babel (Genesis 11:9)
12. d. blessing. (Genesis 27:1–41). Jacob and his mother Rebekah took advantage of Isaac's failing eyesight and frail old age to fool Isaac into giving Jacob the blessing that should have been his brother's.
13. True. (Genesis 9:1) God also gave these instructions to Adam and Eve in Genesis 1:28.
14. The plain of Jordan. Before the destruction of Sodom and Gomorrah, this land was well watered, thus desirable. However, choosing prime land led to Lot's eventual downfall since it brought his family under the influence of sinful Sodom. (Genesis 13:10–13)
15. a. Noah. (Genesis 6:8)
16. This means that Enoch's relationship with God was so close that Enoch was taken alive into heaven.
17. Eden (Genesis 2:8)

18. False. Fearing that they might kill him so they could have the beautiful Rebekah for themselves, Isaac told the men of Gerar that Rebekah was his sister. (Genesis 26:7) When King Abimelech discovered Isaac's lie, he was angry because Abimelech did not want guilt visited upon his men. Abimelech threatened death to any man who touched Rebekah. (Genesis 26:8–11)
19. One, broken into four heads named Pishon, Gihon, Hiddekel (or Tigris), and Euphrates. (Genesis 2:10–14, NKJV)
20. Pharaoh. (Genesis 41:1–7)
21. a. cows and corn. (Genesis 41:2–7) The KJV word "kine" is an old way of saying "cows."
22. Isaac (Genesis 22:9)
23. God confounded their languages so they couldn't understand each other. (Genesis 11:7)
24. c. a bowl of stew and some bread. (Genesis 25:34)
25. False. The last event recorded in the Book of Genesis is Joseph's death. (Genesis 50:26)

MAMMON
1. heart (Matthew 6:21)
2. "Moth and rust doth corrupt, and. . .thieves break through and steal." (Matthew 6:19) Earthly treasures are temporary and susceptible to destruction. Showing others the love of Christ is a treasure stored in heaven and bears eternal rewards.
3. a. he will hate one and love the other.

(Matthew 6:24) No one can serve both God and money, since God's priorities are not those of this world.

4. False. (Luke 16:20–31) Abraham replied, "If they hear not Moses and the prophets, neither will they be persuaded, though one rose from the dead." (Luke 16:31)

5. d. crumbs from his table. (Luke 16:21) The rich man's cruelty to the beggar Lazarus is magnified by his refusal to give Lazarus even the leftovers from his table, which he could have easily spared.

6. a. a drop of water to relieve his torment from the flames of hell. (Luke 16:24) Since Abraham answered on Lazarus's behalf, we can only assume that Lazarus would have shown the rich man mercy in his torment, even though Lazarus was denied crumbs during his life on earth. The gulf between the rich man and Lazarus in heaven and hell is much like the gulf between their earthly positions.

7. The widow contributed two mites, worth about one-eighth of a cent each. (Luke 21:2)

8. b. a strange woman. (Proverbs 5:3–10) The NKJV translates "strange" to be an "immoral" woman.

9. True. The precedent of tithing 10 percent was set by Jacob. (Genesis 28:20–22).

10. c. by sundown. (Exodus 22:26) At that time, clothing also served as a bed at night. Without his clothing, a man would have no bed.

11. "Render therefore unto Caesar the things

which be Caesar's, and unto God the things which be God's." (Luke 20:25)

12. True. (Proverbs 31:20)

13. b. for nothing again. (Luke 6:35) Contrary to the worldly system of wanting payback for every good deed, Jesus admonishes us not to be concerned about our earthly rewards. He points out that sinners loan money to other sinners, which implies that expecting earthly rewards is the way of the sinner. (Luke 6:34)

14. False. They thought the ointment should have been sold and the proceeds given to the poor. (Matthew 26:7–9)

15. Simon tried to buy the gift of God. (Acts 8:18–20)

16. b. searches until she finds it. (Luke 15:8)

17. mammon (Luke 16:13)

18. He was sad because he had many possessions. (Mark 10:22)

19. True. In fact, God gave Job even more possessions than he had previously owned and a new family that included beautiful daughters. (Job 42:12–16)

20. a. thirty pieces of silver. (Matthew 26:14–16)

21. The money is wasted. (Proverbs 29:3)

22. False. (Ecclesiastes 5:10)

23. God. (Deuteronomy 8:18)

24. rich (Proverbs 23:4)

25. False. The love of money is the root of all evil. (1 Timothy 6:10) This verse tells us that wanting others' possessions causes us to fall from the faith, which leads to many sorrows.

JOY

1. True. (Galatians 5:22)
2. The rich farmer wanted to store so much treasure that he would never have to work again. However, he died before his dreams came to pass. This parable illustrates that it is better to lay up our treasures in heaven than on the earth. (Luke 12:19–21)
3. contentment (1 Timothy 6:6)
4. Timothy says the rich should put their trust in the living God, because He will provide their needs. (1 Timothy 6:17)
5. tithes (Malachi 3:10)
6. False. Proverbs 31:30 says, "Favour is deceitful, and beauty is vain: but a woman that feareth the LORD, she shall be praised."
7. reap (Galatians 6:7)
8. c. brutish. (Proverbs 12:1)
9. rejoiceth (Proverbs 13:9)
10. True. (1 Thessalonians 1:6–7)
11. cheerful (2 Corinthians 9:7)
12. Jesus said, "With men it is impossible, but not with God: for with God all things are possible." (Mark 10:27)
13. False. (Matthew 25:24–28)
14. give (Acts 20:35)
15. a. the lilies of the field. (Matthew 6:28–29)
16. a. wisdom. (Ecclesiastes 7:12)
17. d. bride.
18. rubies (Proverbs 31:10)
19. d. purple. (Proverbs 31:22) Since purple dye was very expensive, the color suggests that her thrift has been rewarded with costly

garments. The KJV notes that she wears silk, while the NKJV calls the fabric fine linen. Both suggest wealth.

20. Charity, according to the KJV. Love, in later translations. (1 Corinthians 13:4–7)
21. d. gladness.
22. True. (Acts 8:4–8)
23. servant (Matthew 25:23). These words are the reward of a servant from a joyous master.
24. d. short-lived. (Job 20:5)
25. True. (Luke 15:7)

STORIES JESUS TOLD

1. c. Luke records twenty-seven parables, the most of the four Gospels. Matthew includes twenty, while Mark records nine. The Gospel of John contains no parables.
2. The three types of ground mentioned in the parable of the sower are stony, thorny, and good. (Matthew 13:3–23, Mark 4:2–20, Luke 8:4–15)
3. True. (Mark 4:17) A shallow faith can withstand little trial.
4. b. rock. (Matthew 7:24–27, Luke 6:47–49) Those who build their lives on the Word of God will stand steadfast in time of judgment.
5. word (Mark 4:14)
6. b. worldly cares, riches, and lusts. (Mark 4:18–19)
7. words (Mark 13:31)

8. Like a fishing net, referred to as a dragnet in the NKJV, the kingdom of heaven will gather both good and bad people. They will be sorted out at the time of judgment. (Matthew 13:47–49)

9. False. (Luke 18:4) The judge responded to the widow because he was tired of her pleas. Unlike the judge, the Lord is just, and so He will respond speedily to our prayers. (Luke 18:6–8)

10. One. (Luke 15:10)

11. c. protested angrily to his father for celebrating. (Luke 15: 28–29)

12. c. a job as a hired servant. (Luke 15:19) After losing his fortune, the son was so destitute and friendless that he was willing to take a lowly position in his father's home.

13. savour (Luke 14:34, Matthew 5:13)

14. Jesus. (Luke 15:2)

15. b. watchful for the Son of Man. (Matthew 25:1–13) The foolish virgins were not prepared for the bridegroom's return, so they missed the wedding. We want to be like the five wise virgins, ready for Christ's return. Note Matthew 25:13, which says, "Watch therefore, for ye know neither the day nor the hour wherein the Son of man cometh."

16. Mustard. (Matthew 13:31–32, Mark 4:30–32, Luke 13:18–19)

17. The rich can pay back the meal and hospitality, but the wretched cannot. By doing good to those who cannot return the favor, you will be blessed. (Luke 14:12–14)

18. body (Luke 11:36). A righteous person will convey God's love to others, but a wicked-hearted person cannot because his body is full of darkness.
19. d. sheep, coin, and son. (Luke 15:1–32)
20. False. Although the parable of the prodigal son is probably Jesus' most well-known and popular story, Luke is the only gospel in which it is recorded. (Luke 15:11–32)
21. His enemy planted tares in the field as he slept. (Matthew 13:25)
22. b. the wheat could be uprooted along with the tares. (Matthew 13:29)
23. The Pharisee exalted himself through prayer, while the tax collector humbled himself to God and begged for mercy. (Luke 18:9–14) Jesus reminds us in Luke 18:14, "for every one that exalteth himself shall be abased; and he that humbleth himself shall be exalted."
24. Jesus. (Matthew 21:36–39, Luke 20:13–15) This parable describes how past prophets had been poorly treated and reveals that Jesus knew they would treat Him poorly, even though He is God's son.
25. False. No parables are found in John's Gospel.

A MESSAGE TO THE CHURCHES
1. The Revelation is the last book of the Bible.
2. b. John. (Revelation 1:1–2)
3. Jesus revealed The Revelation to John. (Revelation 1:1–2)
4. True. (Revelation 1:1)

5. b. blessed. (Revelation 1:3)
6. The Revelation addressed seven churches. (Revelation 1:4)
7. Philadelphia. (Revelation 1:11)
8. Pergamum (or Pergamos), Smyrna, Ephesus, Thyatira, Sardis, Philadelphia, Laodicea. (Revelation 1:11)
9. c. Asia Minor. (Revelation 1:4) The KJV simply states, "Asia."
10. False. Jesus is quoted in Revelation 1:8; 1:11; 1:17–3:22; 22:7, 12–13, 16, 20.
11. Alpha (Revelation 1:8)
12. True. Jesus knew the works of all seven churches very well. (Revelation 2:2–4; 2:9; 2:13; 2:19; 3:1; 3:8; 3:15)
13. b. first love. (Revelation 2:4) They had abandoned their love of Jesus to empty rituals.
14. a. tireless labor for Him. (Revelation 2:2–3)
15. The church would be persecuted. Some could expect to be thrown into prison. (Revelation 2:10)
16. life (Revelation 2:10)
17. a. sexually immoral. (Revelation 2:20)
18. False. (Revelation 2:21)
19. Those who had not defiled their garments, i.e., were righteous, were worthy. (Revelation 3:4)
20. True. (Revelation 2:15) The false doctrine of the Nicolaitanes led this church to immoral deeds.
21. b. that they would be delivered from the hour of temptation. (Revelation 3:10)
22. lukewarm (Revelation 3:16). Jesus said this to the church of the Laodiceans.

23. d. wretched, and miserable, and poor, and
     blind, and naked. (Revelation 3:17)
24. a. repent. (Revelation 2:5; 2:16; 2:22; 3:3;
     3:19)
25. Jesus said, "As many as I love, I rebuke and
     chasten: be zealous therefore, and repent."
     (Revelation 3:19)

A NEW CHRISTIAN
BEGINS HIS MINISTRY

1. False. The author is Luke.
2. Saul. (Acts 13:9)
3. True. (Acts 7:58)
4. Saul was on his way to Damascus to find
    Christians. He wanted to bring them in
    bondage to Jerusalem to be punished for
    their faith. (Acts 9:1–2)
5. "Saul, Saul, why persecutest thou me?" (Acts
    9:4)
6. False. Saul trembled and asked Jesus what to
    do. (Acts 9:5–6)
7. d. Straight. (Acts 9:11)
8. "For I will shew him how great things he
    must suffer for my name's sake." (Acts 9:16)
9. d. bear His name to the Gentiles, the kings,
    and the children of Israel. (Acts 9:15)
10. True. (Acts 9:9)
11. Ananias was a disciple in Damascus.
    (Acts 9:10)
12. d. being led by the hands of his traveling
    companions. (Acts 9:8)
13. God (Acts 9:20)

14. d. amazed. (Acts 9:21) They were amazed because they recognized him as a persecutor of Christians, not as a disciple of Christ.

15. a. planning to slay him. (Acts 9:29)

16. The Bible begins to refer to Saul as "Paul" in Acts 13:9, which records the incident where Paul is filled with the Holy Spirit and denounces the sorcerer Bar-Jesus.

17. False. They were forbidden by the Holy Spirit to minister in Asia Minor. (Acts 16:6)

18. b. Troas. (Acts 16:8)

19. a. a vision of a Macedonian man. (Acts 16:9)

20. "These men are the servants of the most high God, which shew unto us the way of salvation." (Acts 16:17)

21. She followed them for many days, making this proclamation. (Acts 16:17–18)

22. Jesus Christ (Acts 16:18)

23. b. have him imprisoned.   (Acts 16:19) They wanted them imprisoned because without her spirit of divination, the girl could no longer make money for them by her fortune-telling.

24. The fortune-teller's masters said that Paul and the other missionaries were Jewish troublemakers who were teaching customs not lawful to Romans. (Acts 16:20–21)

25. False. They sang hymns and prayed. (Acts 16:25)

26. c. sending an earthquake that loosened their bands. (Acts 16:26)

27. c. drew his sword to kill himself. (Acts 16:27)

28. False. They had remained despite their ability to flee. (Acts 16:28)

29. "Sirs, what must I do to be saved?" (Acts 16:30)
30. saved (Acts 16:31)

MIRACLES

1. False. He was swallowed by a big fish. The type of fish is not specified. (Jonah 1:17)
2. Twelve baskets of food were left over after the five thousand were fed. (Matthew 14:20)
3. True. Jesus healed the right ear of the high priest's servant, which had been sliced off by a sword. (Luke 22:51)
4. a. asked Jesus to leave him. (Luke 5:8) This was not a rebuke to the Lord, but a manifestation of Simon Peter's humility since he said, "Depart from me; for I am a sinful man, O Lord."
5. worm (Jonah 4:7)
6. Only one leper thanked Him. (Luke 17:15–19)
7. d. gourd. (Jonah 4:6, 9) The KJV specifies that the plant was a gourd. The NKJV says it was simply a plant, leaving contemporary scholars to make educated guesses as to what type of plant it actually was.
8. Jesus told them to cast their nets again. They caught so many fish that two boats were filled and began to sink. (Luke 5:2–7)
9. Lazarus had been in the tomb four days. (John 11:39)
10. faith (Luke 17:6)

11. d. was afraid they would stone him. (Exodus 17:4)
12. The first miracle of Jesus was His turning water to wine at Cana. (John 2:1–10)
13. False. The sorcerers duplicated the trick, which served God's purpose of hardening Pharaoh's heart. (Exodus 7:11–13)
14. c. ate the other rods. (Exodus 7:12)
15. True. It is generally accepted that each plague was aimed at refuting the worthiness of a specific Egyptian god.
16. The final plague was the deaths of the first-born of every Egyptian family. (Exodus 11:5–6)
17. blood; blood (Exodus 12:13)
18. d. Passover (Exodus 12:14–27)
19. Thomas doubted Jesus' resurrection. (John 20: 24–25)
20. believed; believed (John 20:29)
21. a. the gardener. (John 20:15)
22. Belshazzar the king and everyone at his party saw the handwriting on the wall. (Daniel 5)
23. False. The real offense of Belshazzar was his praise and worship of the gods of silver, gold, brass, iron, wood, and stone as he and his party guests drank out of golden vessels that were taken out of the temple of the house of God. (Daniel 5:3)
24. c. Daniel's God is the living God. (Daniel 6:26)
25. life (John 11:25)